MW01110127

The
Scent *of* Life

A Pocket Prayer Book
by
Michael Anderson

VMI
Publishers

Mike Anderson

Published by

DeepRiver Books

a division of VMI Publishers
Sisters, Oregon
www.vmipublishers.com

ISBN 0-9747190-4-8

DEDICATION

Indebted as I am to the immeasurable joy, original humor, and spontaneous sympathies that seven grandchildren have brought to my life, it is natural to dedicate these words of prayer and hope to them:

Anderson Lee; Taite, Charlie, and Sam Sandefer;
Anna Webb; Kirstin and Ali Barr.

"I get by with a little help from my friends," the Beatles sang. My friends on this project have my continuous thanks: Judy Jones, Bill Carmichael, Lacey Hanes-Ogle, and Melissa Kizer.

TABLE OF CONTENTS

THE SCENT OF LIFE

Live in each season as it passes; breathe the air, drink the drink, taste the fruit, and resign yourself to the influences of each.

Henry David Thoreau

For to me, to live is Christ and to die is gain.

Philippians 1:21

Lord, you are the creator of the earthy aromas of life. Imaginatively, you have given us the pungent memories of events, places and living beings. Thank you for the memory of scent: the clean scent of a baby whose skin is soft as a rose petal...the scent of newly plowed soil.

Each city has its collective scents of individual aromatic signature; Bangkok is different from Beirut, Cape Town and Carmel, Hong Kong and Karachi.

Thank you for the memories of scent: the scent of the horse's neck touched by the rider's face as he whispers "thanks for a great ride"...the scent of the Arizona desert at midnight when the cactus is in bloom...the scent of home-baked cinnamon rolls...the scent of the ocean.

Thank you God for the scent of a woman: my beloved wife of forty-four years, whom I loved, whom you loved. Though painful to recall, I thank you for the memory of the last embrace, moments after she died: her scent of life was gone.

Memories from the sensuous scents of earth—air and sea like the crocuses and daffodils pushing through the last springtime snow—are rich remembrances of life, death, and resurrection. Earth itself is a great, ancient temple filled with the swirling incense of tens of thousands of scents.

Lord, even the memory of imagined scent deepens our love and attraction to the truth of your cosmos. What was the fragrance of the costly perfume a woman poured on the feet of Jesus as she wiped his feet with her hair?

I thank you, God, for the dimensions of love enlarged by the scent of life. Amen.[1]

---

[1] Isaiah 43:13–21: "I am about to do a new thing...do you not perceive it?"
Song of Solomon 2:12–13: "Flowers appear on the earth; the season of singing has come, the cooing of doves is heard in our land. The fig tree forms its early fruit; the blossoming vines spread their fragrance."

HEARING

❧ ❧ ❧ ❧

I'm passionately involved in life. I love its change, its color, its movements. To be able to speak, to see, to hear, to walk, to have music and paintings...it is all a miracle.

Arthur Rubinstein

God of the spoken word, I am humbled, amazed and stunned by the simple fact that the first action, the first verb describing your original act of creation, is the word "said". You said, "Let there be light."[2] You spoke and the cosmos came into being. This grand cosmos has come into being through a power that is to be heard. *Shema*, the Hebrew command to "hear", is the first act of faith.

It is only in hearing that I shall know that you are the Lord who is God and that I can love you with all my heart, soul and mind. The first act of faith does not require action. It simply involves listening to you. You *spoke* the universe into existence. You *spoke* the human

---

[2] Genesis 1:3

spirit into life. You give a simple, finite being like me the capacity to hear your eternal voice. This is an astonishing proposition, Lord.

I cannot hear you when I am listening to the fear-filled voice of my inner consciousness. I cannot hear you when superficial material needs nag me for attention. I cannot hear your voice if I am obsessed with the accumulation of human knowledge.

Hearing, you have taught me, comes first by silence. "Be still and know that I am God," is simple instruction you have given.[3] It is hard to be silent. I need the discipline of detachment...from everything. Lord, will you help me to let go, to surrender and yield? These passive modes are not natural to the habits I have learned that push me to win, to achieve and to succeed.

Perhaps Lord, I could learn from the ebb and flow of nature. I see the way the Canadian Geese hunker down on the shore for the afternoon siesta. It would seem that they are letting the world go by when in reality they are gaining vitality to soar in winds above the world. I must gain vitality of the spirit. In

---

[3] Psalm 46:10

hearing, waiting, listening, resting, you give strength "to mount up with wings like eagles."[4]

Let me hear your words, and when I do, let me obey. Hearing you is the only sound that resonates in harmony in my inner being. I thank you for speaking words of life for hearing. I thank you for becoming the "Word made flesh." Amen.[5]

SEEING

❦ ❦ ❦ ❦

In a dark time, the eye begins to see,
I meet my shadow in the deepening shade;
I hear my echo in the echoing wood –
A lord of nature weeping to a tree.
I live between the heron and the wren,
Beast of the hill and serpents of the den.

Theodore Roethke

---

[4] Isaiah 40:31
[5] Psalms 46:10: "Be still, and know that I am God."
Romans 10:17: "Consequently, faith comes from hearing the message, and the message is heard through the word of Christ."
Deuteronomy 6:4-6: "Hear, O Israel: The Lord our God, the Lord is one."
Matthew 11:15: "He who has ears, let him hear."

It is only with the heart that one can see rightly. What is essential is invisible to the eye.

Antoine de Saint-Exupery

Eternal God, in the mist of the early dawn I begin to see partial outlines and shapes of realities. You remind me of two truths: all my sight-based knowledge is limited, and all my deepest yearning draws me toward you. I am caught lovingly in the soft web of paradox. There is the desire for reasonable truth, and there is deeper yearning for the ultimate truth. You are beyond the space and time that creates the shadows and reflections of all things that live and move and have being. Nevertheless, I believe you, and I believe *in* you.

With physical sight I see the four kinds of entities that make up the visible universe: the inanimate natural objects like the clouds picking up the pinks and blues of the morning sky, the living organisms like the ivy plants growing on the gazebo, the constructed artifacts like the quaint gazebo itself, and all the sentient beings from the great blue heron at the water's edge to humankind.

You have also given me spiritual sight to see the consciousness of your presence with the eyes of the heart. That I should know you and believe in you, I acknowledge, has no more to do with my own initiative than I had to do with causing my own birth. You are the initiator of both our physical birth and our spiritual rebirth.

This day I thank you for the startling gift of faith. I realize the transitory nature of my life and the partiality of my knowledge. You have given me the boldness to walk by faith, not by sight, onto the unknown terrain of the future. This faith is not blind. It is a new way of seeing. Without you, I was blind like the man the Apostle John described who said, "Once I was blind, but now I see, now I believe."[6]

Lord, may I not be blind to the longing and loneliness in others. With the gift of seeing, you have let me see the broken hearts of others. This day I choose to be willing to participate in your love in a loveless world. May I have eyes to see the wonders of your profound grace that heals the sad, the angry, the hopeless, and the broken hearts of many people.

Believing is seeing.   Amen.[7]

---

[6] John 9:25

[7] John 9:30–33: "Now that is remarkable! You don't know where He (Jesus) comes from, yet He opened my eyes. We know that God does not listen to sinners. He listens to the godly man who does His will. Nobody has ever heard of opening the eyes of a man born blind. If this man were not from God, He could do nothing."

TASTING

❀ ❀ ❀ ❀

Happiness quite unshared can scarcely be called happiness; it has no taste.

Charlotte Bronte

The last taste of sweets is sweetest last, Writ in remembrance more than things long past.

William Shakespeare

Lord and God, the creator of savory things, you said, "Taste and see that the Lord is good."[8] Christ invites us to taste life. He took, blessed, broke, and gave us Bread. We remember the taste of the Eucharist in the thankful presence of the Spirit at Confirmation, Maundy Thursday, and at a wedding. We have tasted the glorious presence of your redeeming love. Other memories flood our minds: the last meals we shared with a loved one departed or moved away; a child who married to begin a new home with hearth and table.

Why must we "taste" life in order to see you? May we, existentially, surrender our

---

[8] Psalms 34:8

emotions, intellect, and physical senses and experience your holy presence in the here and now of daily agendas? God of mercy, forgive me for the many times that I have been indifferent to your presence. Indolence and indifference are the parents of my condition of separation. Let me out of the prison of unfeeling. I cannot wait until everything is explained. Not everything can be explained, not even the glorious experience of taste and memory. Wonder and awe are real. You are beyond finding out like a paradox concealed in an enigma surrounded by mystery. And yet, you can be experienced. I want to "taste and see" that you are indeed good.

God, let me not be a fatalist who thinks all things are desperately controlled by an unseen force. Nor do I want to fall again into the narrow and dark valley of the positivist who believes that there is no One to believe. Let me taste the goodness of your covenant of love, and savor you not as law, but as a merciful leader; not as masked power, but in the unmasked love of a true friend. I can taste with awe the Bread of Life.

You are the God in search of humankind.

You pursue me as you sought Adam and Eve in the wasteland east of Eden. When I am exhausted from fleeing your call, thirsty after tasting all the polluted waters of the world, you offer me the spring of water welling up to life. How could I experience this truth unless I am thirsty and willing to taste and see?

Everlasting God, who teaches us to relish life, I thank you for the rich memories of taste. Mother's apple pie, popcorn in tomato soup, Dad's homemade candy, a hot chocolate on a cold winter's night of iceskating on the frozen lake, barbeque ribs at the family picnic, cool clear water after hours of work in blistering heat, heaps of après-baseball ice cream in the park.

Yes Lord, we taste and see that you are the ultimate Living Water that quenches the deep thirst in our souls. Amen.[9]

---

[9] Isaiah 55:1, 6–8: "Come, all you who are thirsty, come to the waters; and you who have no money, come by and eat! Come, buy wine and milk without money and without cost. Seek the Lord while He may be found; call on Him while He is near. Let the wicked forsake His way and the evil man His thoughts. Let him turn to the Lord, and He will have mercy on him, and to our God, for He will freely pardon. For my thoughts are not your thought, neither are your ways my ways," declares the Lord.

TOUCHING

❊ ❊ ❊ ❊

... Jesus himself stood among them and said to them,
"Peace be with you." They were startled and frightened,
thinking they saw a ghost. He said to them, "Why are
you troubled, and why do doubts rise in your minds?
Look at my hands and my feet. It is I myself! Touch
me and see; a ghost does not have flesh and bones, as
you see I have."

Luke 24:36-39

Might I but live to see thee in my touch, I'd say I had
eyes again.

William Shakespeare, King Lear

O Master of the tactile world of life, I
praise your way of meeting us in the mystery
and power of touch.

Isaac wanted to know that Esau was
present. "Let me touch my son."

I remember that night long ago, when as a
child, and I had what seemed like a deadly
dream. Scared, isolated in the deep fears of the
somnolent mind, I awakened to find a strong
arm caressing me, and the voice of my dad
saying, "Everything will be o.k."

And it was.

Lord, thank you for the many times there have been saving touches of friends and family: in the hospital waiting rooms, at memorial services, after failing a board exam, and upon hearing a doctor say, "I am so sorry—we did everything we knew how to do." Indeed, the touch of the silent embrace that followed those words spoke volumes of truth.

Eternal Father, I think I can almost hear the woman's voice in the crowd crying out to Jesus, "If I can just touch his robe, I will be healed." And then she touched his cloak and she was freed from her suffering.[10]   God, you indeed touch us today in our times of broken hearts.

Jesus, you said, "Bring the babies to me," and you touched them. Thank you, God, for the transforming touch of the kingdom of Heaven on earth. If I have the humility to be taught, teach me to touch the realities of faith, hope and love whose verities are within my grasp. I confess my reticence and timidity to touch the "holy other" in the person closest to me. Am I even afraid of touching the real person within me? I see you touching the untouchable who was driven from all contacts with the community. I

---

[10] Luke 8:47

desire the transforming power of touching the truth of life in you, in others, in myself, in this tangible world of beauty. Amen."

ACCEPTING

❖ ❖ ❖ ❖

Accepting the unacceptable transforms and opens up whole new horizons.

Laurel Anderson

God of compassion and grace, the height, breadth, length and depth of your love are infinite. Sometimes I forget the divine dimensions in my little world of finite measurements. I make my world small, as if I'm living in a chrysalis made of my choices of fear, doubt, and resentment. When I choose environments of sounds, sights, and conversations with people who do not have a

---

" Luke 18:15-17: People were also bringing babies to Jesus to have Him touch them. When the disciples saw this, they rebuked them. But Jesus called the children to Him and said, "Let the little children come to me, and do not hinder them, for the kingdom of God belongs to such as these. I tell you the truth, anyone who will not receive the kingdom of God like a little child will never enter it."

purpose-driven life, I find that my own horizons crumple in upon my soul. I thank you for the community of faith, the company of visionaries, and the camaraderie of goodness where confining boundaries are dropped and new experience expands. I sometimes forget to exercise the power I have to choose between the disparate communities of openness or prejudice. Lord, I thank you for shaking the foundations of my complacent world. You have rattled me out of the cocoon of indecision and ignorance. Your Spirit, channeled through spirited people, has done this.

Let me never again choose a road of unbelief. Not accepting your infinite grace and ubiquitous presence leads me to the cynical and dark side of existence that separates me from the Spirit.

In Jesus, you have shown me the power of acceptance. You accept and love me without condition. Today I choose to accept the fact that I am accepted, and I pray that this grace shall infiltrate my life with its power, so that I may be more compassionate with all the life of the cosmos that you love. Let me soar on the thermal updrafts of your spiritual winds that move across the whole earth and sky.

By accepting the indescribable joy that comes from communion with you, may I be ready to accept all the circumstances of life with serenity. Thank you for the peace that passes understanding as a gift from you. Amen.[12]

AGING

❧ ❧

The great thing about getting older is that you don't lose all the other ages you've been.

Madeline L'Engle

God, you are "the same yesterday, today and forever."[13] I change every day. Aging is your gift of life to me. The ages of life have many blessings, though some are realized in retrospect.

In life's first age of innocent dependence,

---

[12] Philippians 4:6–7: "Do not be anxious about anything, but in everything, by prayer and petition, with thanksgiving, present your requests to God. And the peace of God, which transcends all understanding, will guard your hearts and your minds in Christ Jesus."
[13] Hebrews 13:8

you gave me a mother, a father and a familial heritage that reflected your love. I thank you every day for this blessing.

The age of learning, as I see it now in the mirror of memory, was a miracle from heaven. We are living beings created in your image and gifted with billions of brain cells eager for a new experience to store for enduring remembrance. Thank you for the choices of adventures placed before me: adventures with coaches, teachers, mentors, a panoply of uncles, aunts, grandpas and grandmas, who held the compass of your Spirit.

Then came the age of rebellion when you permitted me to learn, unlearn and relearn the way of life. I learned more from failure than success. The crucible of life was essential to the metamorphosis of the soul of my true self. Here I learned the strength of surrender. Your higher power and divine will must exceed my own will. Transformation takes place in the midst of creative chaos.

Gratitude overwhelms me when I consider the amazing age of productivity. When I accept the co-creator work you call me to do, I am privileged to participate with you in a field "white unto the harvest." All of the arts and sciences of our human efforts are empty destinies without your presence. With your presence, we share in the redemption of the world.

With all the gifts of the ages of life, I ask for one more—the gift of the age of wisdom. May I have wisdom to discern your will in the manifold complexities of the human story. May I learn wisdom from you, for you are the source of what is good and true. This day I choose to follow Jesus, the penniless preacher from Nazareth, my wisdom teacher.

In the final age of life, another age of dependence, I will come to you through the doors of death that open not to darkness, but light; not to annihilation, but freedom. My journey in life is not from birth to death; it is from creation to liberation. You are the means and the end of all the ages of life. You are the final age of life. Amen.[14]

---

[14] Matthew 6:25–27: "Therefore I tell you, do not worry about your life, what you will eat or drink; or about your body, what you will wear. Is not life more important than food, and the body more important than clothes? Look at the birds of the air; they do not sow or reap or store away in barns, and yet your heavenly Father feeds them. Are you not much more valuable than they? Who of you by worrying can add a single hour to his life?"

ASPIRING

❧ ❦ ❧

The distant mountains, that uprear
Their solid bastions to the skies;
Are crossed by pathways, that appear
As we to higher levels rise.

The heights by great persons reached and kept
Were not attained by sudden flight,
But they while their companions slept,
Were toiling upward in the night.

Henry Wadsworth Longfellow, The Higher Life

Creator of all life, thank you for the gift of faith to believe in life after birth. There were times when I lived as if I did not believe in the life that was gifted to me. Talents and treasures, loyalties and loves, were wasted, neglected, and abused. If I believe in life after birth, I live with aspiration. Aspiring to gain not substance, not money, not advantageous opportunity: I desire you in my life.

Thank you for giving me a trusting relationship in you. You are the object and subject of my deepest joys and transcending serenity.

God, I desire for you to be in my consciousness so that I may think about you. Be in my conscience so that my behavior shall honor you. Be in my heart so that I may love you. Lord, be in my emotions so that I may rejoice in you. May I look up to the beatific vision of your divine presence in Christ so that you may lift your countenance upon me, and give me your peace.

Loving God, even though you have given me more gifts than I can count, I am bold to ask for one more: the gift of gratitude. You are the Bread of Life. When I come to you, I am never hungry. You alone can fill the emptiness in my soul with the gracious influence of yourself. This undeserved presence is the indefatigable source of my existence. Thank you, my Creator, Redeemer and Comforter. Amen.[5]

---

[5] Numbers 7:24–26: "The Lord bless you and keep you; the Lord make his face shine upon you and be gracious to you; the Lord turn His face toward you and give you peace."

BALANCING

🐛 🐛 🐛 🐛

*What I dream of is an art of balance, of purity and
serenity devoid of troubling or depressing subject
matter...a soothing, calming influence on the mind.*

Henri Matisse

*Each of you should look not only to your own interests,
but also to the interests of others. Your attitude should
be the same as that of Christ Jesus: Who, being in very
nature God, did not consider equality with God
something to be grasped, but made himself nothing,
taking the very nature of a servant, being made in human
likeness.*

Philippians 2:4–7

Lord of life, I live in a world where justice
is in jeopardy. I pray for a changed world
where people experience balance, especially the
balance of power and justice. At times I have
wanted more power for myself. You have
shown me, O Lord, that I could not be free
without justice. I imagine a new earth in which
the just people may not be dispossessed of
power, and where the powerful people may be
just.

You revealed the balancing of power and moral right in Christ, who never compromised justice for popularity or privilege. His justice is hard, not because it is not completely loving, but because it is costly. I want justice to be easy and without sacrifice. I am, nevertheless, aware that all justice in the community, nation and world that I experience, has come from sacrificial living of others. Christ, your Son, died that I may live. You have created in me a heart that is restless in the presence of injustice. You have shown us what is right to do. Justice is love in action. This Christ-like love unveils the face of evil. Evil hates justice and raises its ugly head wherever good is done, because evil loves power without justice. Thank you for showing us the balance of power and justice in Jesus. The final victory over evil is won, not through retaliation, but through reconciliation. You have vindicated the sacrificial lives of many who served others with the supreme goodness of justice. Your grace is amazing. I rejoice in it.

Lord, I confess that without you, "Life's but a walking shadow, a poor player, that struts and frets his hour upon the stage, and then is heard no more; it is a tale told by an idiot, full of sound and fury, signifying nothing."[16]

When my life is invested in the balancing virtue of your will, you give me the courage to take a moral inventory of myself.

Loving Lord, will you help me to balance my power to love with those in this time and place who are rendered powerless? Only then can I be in balance in your scales of justice. Amen.[17]

BELIEVING

🌱 🌱 🌱 🌱

Man is what he believes.

Anton Chekhov

I was wandering like a lost sheep, searching outside of myself for that which was within. I ran through all the streets and squares of this great city, the world, searching for Thee, O God, and I found Thee not, because I sought Thee wrongly. Thou wert within me

---

[16] William Shakespeare, Macbeth, Act 5, sc. 5, 1.16

[17] Jeremiah 22:3: "Do what is just and right."

Micah 6:8: "He has showed you, O man, what is good. And what does the Lord require of you? To act justly and to love mercy and to walk humbly with your God."

and I sought Thee without.

St. Augustine, Soliloquies

Eternal God, help me to accept the projective power of believing. True belief opens doors. You, O Lord, are the source of my belief. You create new vistas for the eyes of faith. Let me doubt my doubts, and believe my beliefs, all the while thanking you that believing is a doorway to knowledge.

Believing hearts are courageous hearts. You have said that if I believe, even though I die, I shall live. Because I must put to death all things that steal life from me, I accept the power of resurrection in your love that overcomes death. You are "the resurrection and the life."[18]

What I believe, I become. Therefore, let me believe in the real, the true, and the just hope of the world. I confess that when I refuse to believe in something, I am prone to believe in anything that comes my way. Let me learn how to respond to my inner cynic, pessimist and inquisitor. May I believe in the affirmations of life and receive forgiveness for the unbelief that repels the gracious gifts of life.

You have said, "Choose this day who you

---

[18] John 11:25

will serve." I choose to believe in you, in your justice and providence in history. I choose not to believe in self−aggrandizing power, wealth, and the retributive morality of doing unto others as they do unto me.

May I accept the simple belief that Jesus taught. If you, God, are God indeed, should I not believe that you care for me and all others much more than you care for the flowers of the fields? Can I not see that the lilies of the field are more beautiful than the rich person's splendid wealth? I need not worry nor be anxious if I believe in the kingdom of God as my first priority, and accept all that shall be given by you, one day at a time. Amen.[19]

BELONGING

🦎 🦎 🦎 🦎

Just as the wave cannot exist for itself, but must always participate in the swell of the ocean, so we can never experience life by ourselves, but must always share the

[19] Joshua 24:15 and 23–24: Joshua said, "But as for me and my household, we will serve the Lord. Now then, throw away the foreign gods that are among you and yield your hearts to the Lord, the God of Israel." And the people said to Joshua, "We will serve the Lord our God and obey Him."

experience of life that takes place all around us.
Albert Schweitzer, My Faith

What life have you if you have not life together? There is no life that is not in community, and no community not lived in praise of God.
T. S. Eliot, The Rock

Eternal God, as I listen to the songs in the hearts of others, and in my own, many are sad. There is a deep yearning in the human community to belong to one whose power is greater than our own. Saint Augustine cried out, "Our hearts are restless until they rest in Thee." We are groundless until we belong to you. We are not ultimately comfortable when we are isolated from others. We need to experience the vitality of life that is connected in love to you and to others. Like marble in the master sculptor's hand crying out for shape and refinement, so my life calls out for the contours and forms of your creative influence.

When I belong to you, I am released from my captivity to the dark and destructive powers. I am not free to be until I am willing to belong.

Not one follower of your truth can walk in the truth alone. Within the community to which we belong, we find the truth that sets us free.

Thank you for the strength of the church that has been a place to belong throughout the ages. Thank you for the sinews of faith that bind us together. Together we experience the Spirit. The surprising variety of modes exhibiting love, joy and peace, the signs of unusual holy presence, arise from the unlikely, the unexpected, the common and extraordinary members of your community.

Today I promise to reach out to someone who desires to belong but feels shunned, rejected, or disconnected from others.

Today, I thank you for coming into my life and giving me the assurance of belonging to the companions of the way who is Jesus Christ. Amen.[20]

---

[20] John 15:4–5: "Remain in me, and I will remain in you. No branch can bear fruit by itself; it must remain in the vine. Neither can you bear fruit unless you remain in me. I am the vine; you are the branches. If a man remains in me and I in him, he will bear much fruit; apart from me you can do nothing."

BIRTHING

It was the rainbow gave thee birth,
And left thee all her lovely hues.

W.H. Davies, *Kingfisher*

Man is born to live, not to prepare for life.

Boris Pasternak, *Dr. Zhivago*

Not in utter nakedness, but trailing clouds of glory do
we come from God, who is our home.

William Wordsworth,
Ode on Intimations of Immortality

Eternal Creator, you bring life and truth into being through birthing, through love, through pain, and through struggle. Today I contemplate the mystery of new life.

I thank you that I am alive, and do not forget the birthing into life through my mother. I thank you for her selfless love. You gave her instincts of Christ-like kindness. I am grateful for a dad who showed that discipline is the doorway to freedom. Supremely, I thank you for the new birth in the Spirit and faith in Christ.

Scripture teaches us that your whole

creation comes into being through birthing tension like a mother birthing a child. The new reality of your kingdom on earth "has been groaning as in the pains of childbirth." Truth, love, and justice are not easy, passive or apathetic. The new creation's birthing is painful, cataclysmic, hopeful, and real.

Let me not forget the birthing of Jesus into this world. In Him I see your truth revealed through conflict, suffering, and death. Mary's relentless hope and humble acceptance of your will in the composite world of goodness and evil, give me inspiration and courage.

The birth of the new image of Christ in me was not without pain and recognition of death. The old order of life, which has turned away from truth, must die so that the new birth in your grace may come.

This new birth is the new beginning of the new being of an abundant life in a cosmos of limitless horizons. I praise you for the spirit and the new birth. Amen.[21]

---

[21] Romans 8:20–22: "For the creation was subjected to frustration, not by its own choice, but by the will of the one who subjected it, in hope that the creation itself will be liberated from its bondage to decay and brought into the glorious freedom of the children of God. We know that the whole creation has been groaning as in the pains of childbirth right up to the present time."

BURNING

✤ ✤ ✤ ✤

O burning mountain, O chosen sun, O perfect moon,
O fathomless well, O unattainable height, O clearness
beyond measure, O wisdom without end. O mercy
without limit, O strength beyond resistance, O crown of
all majesty, the humblest you created sings your praise.
Mechthild of Magdeburg

Someday, after we have mastered the winds, the waves
and gravity, we shall harness for God the energies of
love. Then, for the second time in the history of the
world, man will have discovered fire.
Teilhard de Chardin

Spirit of the Living God, hear my prayer.
Sometimes my soul feels like bleached bones
lying under the desert sun. Where is the sign
of life? Give me the faith of an Ezekiel to believe
that the burning bones of my spiritual being may
be brought life.

Your Spirit has the power to raise me up in
the form of a life filled with purpose. I recognize
that the desert experience is necessary for
elemental change to come about. You are
burning away the dross and behaviors that were

shackles on my life. Now, these dry bones are ready to walk around, shout aloud and celebrate transformation through your Spirit.

I am ready for the new. The fire of life, the fire of courage and the fire of justice are the burning desires of the new being you create. Each day, whether I see it or not, the great engine star you have created for this heliocentric solar system is burning and giving the energy from which all things on this planet, great and small, take life. Whether I see it or not, your Great Spirit is a burning fire that gives me the energy of love, joy, peace, patience, kindness and self-control. I pray that my heart may be an altar and thy Spirit may be the flame.

Give me wisdom to understand the larger "burnings" of life. Like lightning strikes leaping into massive forest fires that burn away the bramble thickets to prepare the way for new wild flowers, the fires of your justice prepare human history for the new humanity in Christ.

At last Lord, let me see the burning light that makes the entire landscape of humankind an infinite day. Amen.[22]

---

[22] Ezekiel 37:3-6: I said, "O Sovereign Lord, you alone know." Then He said to me, "Prophesy to these bones and say to them, dry bones, hear the word of the Lord! This is what the Sovereign Lord says to these bones: I will make breath enter you, and you will come to life. I will attach tendons to you and make flesh come upon you and cover you with skin; I will put breath in you, and you will come to life. Then you will know that I am the Lord."

CONTINUING

❊ ❊ ❊ ❊

We must not hope to be mowers, and to gather the ripe gold ears, unless we have first been sowers and watered the furrows with tears. It is not just as we take it, this mystical world of ours, life's field will yield as we make it a harvest of thorns or of flowers.

Johann Wolfgang von Goethe

If ye continue in my word, then are ye my disciples indeed.

John 8:31 (KJV)

God, you are the Eternal Now whom I meet in your creation. Your continuing creation is filled with mystery and the discoverable. You are the One before and after all things. You are the creator of quasars, gluons and quarks. You are the designer of neurons, neutrons and the awe–filled numinous. You are the innovator of light, leptons and the mystery of love.

You give me the joy and zeal to use the tools of faith and reason, of hope and science. Give me humility to see that everything in this world has changed, except your grace. I too, must grow, must change, in thought and action.

Yesterday shall never return; tomorrow is only a projected vision. Today I live in the motion of the river of life. It moves through quiet inlets, in narrow rapids, and over waterfalls. You are the same "yesterday, today, and forever."[23]

I seek guidance for this path from birth through death to you.

Give me a mind and heart to appreciate the connectedness of all life, to enlarge the circle of understanding other people, to deepen the experience of wisdom, to discover more and more of my self, and to be loyal to the direction of the inner compass of your will.

Thank you for this moment in life. Amen.[24]

DOWNSIZING

❋ ❋ ❋ ❋

Christian simplicity is the very perfection of the interior life – God, His will and pleasure as its sole object.
Jean Nicolas Grou, *The Hidden Life of the Soul*

---

[23] Hebrews 13:8
[24] Psalms 119:41–45 (NRSV): "Let your steadfast love come to me, O Lord, your salvation according to your promise. Then I shall have an answer for those who taunt me, for I trust in your word...I will keep your law continually, forever and ever. I shall walk at liberty, for I have sought your precepts."

Beneath the crude shell of materialism there lies in most persons an innate longing for the spiritual and the eternal.

John LaFarge, *An American Dream*

God of all time, matter and energy; Lord of the universe and Creator of microcosms; let me commune with you about the size of my place in the reality of life.

When I doubt what you can or shall do, I am saying that my God is too small. Often I have envisioned myself too large with my frenzied activities and my desires for accumulation of material things. You are the Great God who is the light of the world. Can anyone see your light through the opaqueness of my life?

I am the one who needs to downsize. I need to de-emphasize desires, postpone gratifications, discipline appetites, and make space and time for enlarging the realm of love and holy presence in my life.

I meditate upon Christ. He had no trust fund, no endowment, no institutional position of power, no popular front organization. He chose to downsize his divine prerogatives and took on the form of a servant of humanity. In his humility, there is infinite power. In his apparent weakness, there is overwhelming strength. In his death, there is resurrection to eternal life.

In downsizing desires, acquisitions, and self-focused attention, may I let your love increase, the love that is boundless in this brief history of time. Help me Lord, to enlarge the spiritual habitat of your will and diminish my own. I pray with John the Baptist, "He must become greater; I must become less." Amen.[25]

DYING

❀ ❀ ❀ ❀

Death...is no more than passing from one room into another. But there's a difference for me, you know. Because in that other room I shall be able to see.

Helen Keller

Lord of life, death and eternal life. I meditate on the meaning of dying. Sometimes dying seems serene and balanced with

---

[25] John 3:30; Galatians 2:20: "I have been crucified with Christ and I no longer live, but Christ lives in me. The life I live in the body, I live by faith in the Son of God, who loved me and gave himself for me."

harmony...the old elephant walking over the last horizon, alone...the golden retriever's knowing eyes looking into my own as he accepts the end-time of an abundant life...the wind blown Cyprus tree defeated and uprooted on a beach after the perfect storm...the beloved spouse laughing, smiling and giving stout-hearted wisdom to her family in the waning hours of her life.

Lord God, how can it be that I should learn about *life* from the experiences of *death*? The paradox of painfulness and illumination, of communal love and desperate isolation, brings me close to your Spirit. The Spirit that raised Christ from death teaches me that Jesus endured the cross "because of the joy he knew would be his afterward."[26] I cannot explain the dichotomy of life and death. I can believe and experience the resurrection. Dying is a prelude to living; crucifixion precedes resurrection. "The seed put into the ground first dies and than grows hundred fold."[27] Dying to powers of destruction in my life, may I discover the undying transformational power of your eternal love.

You teach me not only in words of wisdom,

---

[26] Hebrews 12:2 NLT
[27] John 12:24

but in the flesh and blood of a person, Jesus of Nazareth, which heightens my understanding of dying and living. Not all dying is necessary or acceptable...horrific accidents, death camps, killing fields, deadly passions and deadly diseases. Experiencing more and more of the vicissitudes and ambiguities of living, I am sensitized to participate with you, God, in the world where your "kingdom comes as it is in heaven," beyond the veil of tears, beyond the dying. Amen.[28]

ECSTACY

❀ ❀ ❀ ❀

No eye has seen, no ear has heard, and no mind has imagined what God has prepared for those who love him.

I Corinthians 2:9

The soul should always stand ajar, ready to welcome the ecstatic experience.

Emily Dickinson

---

[28] Romans 8:11: "And if the Spirit of Him who raised Jesus from the dead is living in you, He who raised Christ from the dead will also give life to your mortal bodies through his Spirit, who lives in you."

Eternal God of all beings and existence, you come to us as a "still, small voice," as an echo in the morning mist across a sea in Galilee, in the voice of a prophet exiled in a friendless foreign land. You come to us. If and when we hear your voice, we find for the first time, the true source of truth, and the experience is ecstasy. Your presence is exciting.

Thank you for giving us words from many languages of the world to understand ourselves, the universe, and the nature of faith. From the Greeks we have the word *ekstatikos*, "ecstatic", literally "getting out-of-the status quo." The ex-status quo is exciting, for you have created us to seek adventure.

God, I confess that ecstasy has been both a source of my doom as well as my divine rebirth. When I seek ecstasy in outward things to answer the inner void, I become addicted to false gods who promise vacuous fulfillments. The true adventure you give to me through an exciting faith allows me to walk the journey of life, not by coerced law, but motivated by loving trust. When the mind and heart meet with truth, adventure, and new discovery, the exciting moment is filled. It is rapturous, overpowering, intense and poetic. It is the delightful contemplation of divine displacement.

Ecstasy has been a part of both my faith and my folly. Foolishly, I tried many ways to get out of the meaninglessness of the status quo. You distracted me, and disrupted the axis of my self-made world. Thank you for showing me the way to the "ecstatic" movement that heals brokenness, fills emptiness, converts fearfulness to faithfulness. The endless pursuits of ecstatic folly followed a path into the abyss. The ecstatic faith to accept you as the true source of life becomes the exciting experience of divine love. Amen.[29]

---

[29] The Letter to Jewish Christians 1:1-4 from The NT in Modern English by J. B. Phillips: "God, who gave to our forefathers many different glimpses of the truth in the words of the prophets, has now, at the end of the present age, given us the truth in the Son. Through the son God made the whole universe, and to the Son he has ordained that all creation shall ultimately belong. This Son, radiance of the glory of God, flawless expression of the nature of God, himself the upholding principle of all that is, effected in person the reconciliation between God and man and then took his seat at the right hand of the majesty on high — thus proving himself, by the more glorious name that he has won, far greater than all the angels of God."
1 Peter 1:8-9: "Though you have not seen Him, you love Him; and even though you do not see Him now, you believe in Him and are filled with an inexpressible and glorious joy, for you are receiving the goal of your faith, the salvation of your souls."

FORGIVING

※ ※ ※ ※

Forgiveness is the essence of the gospel.

Martin Luther

The hatred which divides nation from nation, race from race, class from class.
        Father, forgive...
The pride which leads to trust in ourselves and not in God.
        Father, forgive...

Coventry Cathedral Prayer

God of the everlasting waters of forgiveness, wash me clean. You have demonstrated to all of history your forgiving heart. Jesus taught us to pray daily that we shall be forgiven as *we forgive*. In Jesus we see the essence of the gospel is forgiveness.

I admit to stumbling on this rock of truth. Can I freely forgive others, all other persons: "forgive us our sins as we forgive those who sin against us"? One of my sins is the unwillingness (or is it the incapacity?) to forgive all others.

There is a refreshing release in forgiveness. When I do forgive others, I am released from their negative hold on me. Accepting the fact that you accept me releases me from the heavy burden of regrets. When I do accept forgiveness—from you, from others—I feel the lightness of the new air that leads me outward on the wings of opportunities. Then your love is present and life is reborn.

When I admit all my needs to you—all my shortcomings, all my failed attempts to live life faithfully—your mercy is from everlasting to everlasting. You do not forgive me for the short term, but forever. Thank you. You have made forgiveness the strongest link in the golden chain of love. The experience of forgiving one another is the linkage of my life to family, friends and colleagues on life's journey through the jungles of imperfection.

When I am caught up with retributive justice, vindictiveness, and blame for others, let me see two things more clearly: my incompleteness, and the vision of Christ forgiving those who crucified him.

You have shown us what is true. Forgiveness opens the door to freedom. For freedom Christ set us free. Amen.[30]

---

[30] Colossians 3:12–14: "Therefore, as God's chosen people, holy and dearly loved, clothe yourselves with compassion, kindness, humility, gentleness and patience. Bear with each other and forgive whatever grievances you may have against one another. Forgive as the Lord forgave you. And over all these virtues put on love, which binds them all together in perfect unity."

INTROSPECTING

● ● ● ●

The virtue of wisdom more than anything else contains a divine element which always remains.

Plato, *The Republic*

The most beautiful experience we can have is the mysterious. It is the fundamental notion that stands at the cradle of true art and true science.

Albert Einstein, *Ideas and Opinions*

The simplicity of the gospels makes false mysticism impossible. Christ has delivered us forever from the esoteric and the strange. He has brought the light of God to our own level to transfigure our ordinary existence.

Thomas Merton

Eternal God, Lord of all humankind, I am unmasked by the test of history. Time will tell. If I am aware of history's lessons, I learn that I cannot live fully a self-determined life. Such a conceit about selfhood, for me, is like boating under a full sail with no keel and no rudder. Without the ballast and balance of faith, without the wind power of your Spirit, I am lost at sea. Your wisdom helps me to understand the heavy seas, the tides of time, and the destructive vortexes of the deep.

Without the leading of your truth I misunderstand even my own motivations. Rudeness and aggression may be an imitation of weakness and fear. Persistence may be disguised stubborn indecision. Obtuse profundity may be a shadow hiding the sense of lost understanding. Without your truth about life, history, self, and community, I may even forget the simplest fact: with one exception, the entire population of the world consists of *others*. I am not the center of life or world history.

Is it true that other people mirror our selves? The power of choice in the attitude emanating from me surprises me. The attitude I project collects an environment I experience. If I live day by day with resentment, I collect about myself a coterie of unhappy people who are bitter about the direction of history and life. If I live with the joy in my heart that Jesus had in his, I discover that cheerfulness is not a placebo but a reality. Thank you, Lord God, for revealing to us the grace of Christ that is out of all proportion to the evil in the world. All wrongs do not compare to his right. Your love vastly exceeds all negativities in all time and in all places of the universe.

May I accept with humility and courage the circumstances that surround my life. Today, I choose to change what in your light should be changed, and accept what in truth cannot be changed, with acquiescence to your divine mercy and justice in the affairs of the human story. Amen.[31]

LEARNING

There are many truths of which the full meaning cannot be realized until personal experience has brought it home.

John Stuart Mill

See how the unlearned start up and take heaven by storm whilst we with all our learning grovel upon the earth.

St. Augustine of Hippo, *Confessions*

---

[31] Psalms 90:12: "Teach us to number our days aright, that we may gain a heart of wisdom."

God, you came to us as a *rabbi*, a teacher. The first persons to accept you were *disciples*, learners. I have very much to learn. If you continue to be my rabbi, I want to be your disciple. In learning, I must be willing to risk failure. In learning, I must be able to see change for good when it occurs in others, especially the beloved closest to me. I may learn from everybody. From the talkative; I learn silence. From the rude; I learn civility. From the heartless; I learn kindness.

Help me, O God, to learn that humble wisdom is more important than many facts. I must confess that what I think I already know can sometimes prevent me from learning what is new. When I face the potential of new truth, help me to be willing to unlearn and relearn.

There are two vast universes of being I yearn to learn more about. One is the mystery of you, Father, Son and Holy Spirit. The other is me. I know very little about myself. I "see but a poor reflection as in a mirror."[32] I may continue to learn about the personhood you and the whole creation have formed in the intricate web of life.

---

[32] 1 Corinthians 13:12

48

I long, "as a deer longs for streams of water," to learn from the Advocate who "will teach us everything." Thank you, Lord and Teacher, for giving us minds to learn as long as we live, and creating within us hearts to learn of love. Amen.[33]

PRAYING

God, grant me the serenity
to accept the things I cannot change,
courage to change the things I can,
and the wisdom to know the difference.

Living one day at a time,
Enjoying one moment at a time,
Accepting hardship as the pathway to peace;
Taking, as He did, this sinful world
as it is, not as I would have it;
Trusting that He will make all things right

---

[33] John 14: 25–27: Jesus said, "All this I have spoken while still with you. But the Counselor, the Holy Spirit, whom the Father will send in my name, will teach you all things and will remind you of everything I have said to you. Peace I leave with you; my peace I give you. I do not give to you as the world gives. Do not let your hearts be troubled and do not be afraid."

if I surrender to His will;
That I may be reasonably happy in this life,
and supremely happy with Him
Forever in the next.
Amen.

Reinhold Niebuhr

Eternal God, Creator and Redeemer of life, I humbly thank you for the mystery of this momentous moment. I am praying. I cannot fully explain this experience to anyone who has not experienced prayer, nor can I explain love to anyone who has never been loved.

Is it that we are indeed "created in your image" that the ineffably sublime presence of your loving and holy being becomes a part of our deepest consciousness if we stand still in awe and wonder?

Give us this day our daily wonderment.

Miracles are with me each day as the earth is bathed in sunlight. If I come into the open from behind the walls of self-concentration, perhaps then I can see. Let me not look down like Narcissus who gazed into his own image until drowning in fascination with himself. I must look up to the highest power and glory, to you the Almighty God, you the loving Christ, and the comforting Holy Spirit.

I searched for you in human constructions, in human institutions, in religious symbols and organized liturgies. I searched for you as the reasonable word that completes a logical syllogism. I did not find you at the conclusion of a mathematical equation, but I do find you in the equation of love. You were pursuing me. You found me. I was searching for you in a limited world. But you were not lost. I was. I looked for the One who is before, above and beyond knowledge in the limited world of reason. Then I discovered the sage's advise: "The heart has its reasons of which reason knows nothing."[34]

You are the One who is "majestic in holiness, awesome in glory working wonders," if I surrender to faith that allows me to see.[35]

You have become the living Spirit that fills my empty heart. "Our hearts are restless until they find rest in Thee."[36] Without reason, my belief is blind; without faith, my reason is impaired.

For friends, family and faith in Christ; I thank you God. May I pause before the simple astonishments of life in reverence for your blessings, for food, water, fruit, wine, and the nourishing companionship of others. Every

[34] Blaise Pascal, "Pensees"
[35] Exodus 15:11
[36] St. Augustine

thing good comes from you, including the joy of communion in prayer. Amen.[37]

RAISING

∼ ∼ ∼ ∼

Christ has turned all our sunsets into dawns.
Clement of Alexandria

The resurrection is the beginning of God's great act of redemptive transformation, the seed from which the new creation begins to grow.

John Polinghorne,
Cambridge Professor of Mathematical Physics

Therefore, if anyone is in Christ, he is a new creation; the old has gone, the new has come!

2 Corinthians 5:17

God of infinite wisdom and unqualified compassion, miracles surround me and I miss most of what happens. Even when it is as obvious as the ground upon which I walk, the person with whom I talk, the sky whose light I

---

[37] Matthew 6:9-13: Jesus said, "This, then is how you should pray: Our Father in heaven, hallowed be your name, your kingdom come, your will be done on earth as it is in heaven. Give us today our daily bread. Forgive us our debts, as we also have forgiven our debtors. And lead us not into temptation, but deliver us from the evil one."

use, miracles often elude me. Sensitize me Lord, make me aware of your power of raising me from death to life. You raised Christ to life again from "the agony of death, because it was impossible for death to keep its hold on Him."[38]

I have been, at times, like the first disciples who heard about the resurrection and the story "seemed to them like nonsense."[39] When death has consumed my love and locked me behind the doors of fear and loss, such stories of raising the dead seemed like an illusion wrapped in a fantasy. Then, you broke through those doors where I was shackled in death's throes. You turned many days of sunsets into dawns. Death is transformed to life again. Resurrection is here and now. It was not necessary for you to prove to me the stories of raising others from the dead. You, the living Mediator, the resurrected One himself, raised me from certain death.

Eternal Lord, thank you for raising me to life again. I can now humbly say with the Apostle, "once I was dead, but now I live." There are many things in my life that must die, in order that I may truly live. Unmitigated self-

---

[38] Acts 2:24
[39] Luke 24:11

53

centeredness, obsession with outward appearances on the human scale, fears about fate controlling the future, the heavy burden of the residuals from the pursuit of immediate gratification—all of these must die. Your Spirit, that raised Christ from death, is now raising me to new life. The past is forgiven. I am released. The future is insured by providential love. I live without fear. The present is a pathway lighted by the word. I walk by faith. God, in raising us from death to life, you have given us the secure bridge from expectation to fulfillment.

Your gift of this persistent springtime within the human condition is a cosmic event that changes for good all of life and all of history. Glory shall be unto you our God, unto Christ our Savior, unto the Spirit our Guide. Amen.[40]

---

[40] Mark 16:9: "When Jesus rose early on the first day of the week, He appeared first to Mary Magdalene, out of whom He had driven seven demons. She went and told those who had been with Him and who were mourning and weeping. When they heard that Jesus was alive and that she had seen Him, they did not believe it."
Luke 24:11: "But they did not believe the women, because their words seemed to them like nonsense."
Colossians 3:1: "Since, then, you have been raised with Christ, set your hearts on things above, where Christ is seated at the right hand of God."

RECEIVING

❖ ❖ ❖ ❖

*You are accepted, accepted by that which is greater than
you...Do not try to do anything now; perhaps later you
will do much. Do not seek for anything; do not perform
anything; do not intend anything. Simply accept the fact
that you are accepted...We cannot compel anyone to
accept himself. But sometimes it happens that we receive
the power to say "yes" to ourselves...grace has come
upon us.*

Paul Tillich, Union Seminary, NYC,
"Shaking the Foundations"

God of the gifts of life, I confess my
hesitancy and inconsistency about one of the
most powerful actions of life. I want to be
proactive, co-creative, and an initiator of
thought and work; however, you are asking me
to be passive, humble, quiet and open-handed.
You have said that Christ, grace, Spirit, and love
are to be received. I find it easier to give love
than receive love. Master teachers of life have
taught me that to be fully human; I must give and
receive love.

When I am in the posture of receiving gifts
from your hand through other people, am I

afraid of exposing my vulnerability? Do I fear that I shall lose control? Am I afraid of accepting the fact that I am accepted? Your grace can only be known and experienced when I let go, and receive what you give.

When I consider your truth revealed through women and men of complete virtue and simple courage, I see that often times they were repelled, rebuffed and refused by people they loved. Was the message of love, joy and peace an affront to people of power, prestige and privilege? It is hard to receive the gift of truth when we feel that we have earned the valuable assets of life.

There comes a time, Lord, when I cannot live from the resources of my self-made storehouse of treasure. It is never enough. I never have enough of the things that are unnecessary. When I hunger for you and thirst after your way of life, I am confronted with the axiom: You are love. I must receive love, receive Christ, and receive the Spirit. It is in the recognition of my emptiness that I am ready to receive and be filled. It is not my doing. It is your giving that fills the empty vessel of my life. I receive grace, just as I am, not after my attempt at moral modification. Without pretense, without cost, without ritual, without human effort, you give yourself in love to me. Receiving love is the beginning of my transformation. Like a newborn baby, life is given me. As a baby, my first act of new life is breathing in fresh air of life.

Today I shall begin life like a newborn person receiving your love. Amen.[41]

REFLECTING

It's wonderful to climb the liquid mountains of the sky. Behind me and before me is God and I have no fears.
Helen Keller

There is no good in trying to be more spiritual than God. God never means man to be a purely spiritual creature...He likes matter. He created it.
C. S. Lewis, *Mere Christianity*

---

[41] John 1:12: "Yet to all who received Him, to those who believe in His name, He gave the right to become children of God."

Almighty God whose mystery lies beyond the reach of all imaginations of humankind, I thank you for reflecting your image in "the face of Jesus."

You are the eternal source of all life. You care for us as a Good Shepherd, a wise mentor, the model of beauty, and a teacher of truth. The best of our arts and sciences seek the profound creativity of your patterns of life.

When I am reflecting upon your revealing light, I acknowledge that my incompleteness, brokenness and sorrow are often the places you illuminate with soft rays of hope and courage. Sometimes your love is carried by a friend, or beloved member of the family. There are times a stranger, as an angel in disguise, is the messenger of loving light.

Lord, I am a pilgrim on a journey that evolves before me. I have a sense of destiny which I do not perfectly see. You are reflecting the light of guidance as a "lamp for my feet," one step at a time, one day at a time. You have given the gift of optimism that this road I travel is not destined to oblivion. It leads to you, the Creator and Redeemer of life, the Source–Light of the world. Amen.[42]

REMEMBERING

Remember the sky you were born under. Know each star's stories. Remember the moon, know who she is. Remember the sun's birth at dawn that is the strongest point of time. Remember sundown, and the giving away to night. Remember your birth, how your mother struggled to give you form and breath. You are evidence of her life, and her mother's, and hers. Remember your father, his hands cradling your mother's heart. He is your life also.

Remember the earth, whose skin you are. Red earth, yellow earth, white earth, brown earth, black earth, we are earth. Remember the plants, trees, animal life, who all have their own tribes, their families their histories, too. Talk to them, listen to them, they are alive poems. Remember the wind, remember her voice, she knows the origin of this universe. Remember that you

---

[42] 2 Corinthians 4:6: For God, who said, "Let light shine out of darkness," made His light shine in our hearts to give us the light of the knowledge of the glory of God in the face of Christ.

are all people, and that all people are you.

Remember that you are this universe, and this universe is you.

Remember all is in motion, is growing, is you.

Remember that language comes from this.

Remember the dance that language is, that life is.

Remember

To remember.

Joy Harjo, Native American

Gracious God, I thank you for the gift of remembering.

Let me remember *to* remember.

Remembering the gentle love of my father as he carried my mother in his strong arms from the car to her bed where she could rest and recover from surgery; I thank you for the recollection. I remember his story about her cancer, the surgery, and instruction that all the members of the family must share the work she had done. I remember his prayers. I remember her joyous presence in the nascent passages of time allotted my life. Thank you.

There are poignant remembrances of your grace from times when my own actions separated me from doing your love and justice, while I tried to fill the void in my life with substitutes for truth. You have shown me the way to Christ-like love. Remembering that His passion is not given without sacrifice, I know Christ's priceless love is given without cost to me. Remembering my redemption overwhelms me with gratitude.

Thank you for the memories of a phalanx of persons united in the common good of the human community. Their wealth, work, and wisdom create a place for the tree of life, from which I take fruit to grow and yield its harvest.

Thank you for the freedoms I experience in a nation whose history is marked by a few great people of vision and compassion. Let me remember to remember the sacrifice of thousands who have made this extraordinary encounter with liberty a part of my consciousness.

Remembering that you gave your Son "because you loved the world," let me never doubt that you are the Good Shepherd for all people everywhere.

Most of all, I remember your amazing creation, your tender kindness, your subtle providence, and your loving redemption of humanity. Amen.[43]

REPENTING

🎜 🎜 🎜 🎜

Jesus said, "I tell you that in the same way there will be more rejoicing in heaven over one sinner who repents than over ninety-nine righteous persons who do not need to repent."

Luke 15:7

I can take less than a minute to commit a sin. It takes not as long to obtain God's forgiveness. Penitence and amendment should take a lifetime.

Hubert van Zeller

We shall have to repent in this generation, not so much for the evil deeds of the wicked people, but for the appalling silence of the good people.

Martin Luther King

---

[43] John 3:16-17: "For God so loved the world that He gave His one and only Son, that whoever believes in Him shall not perish but have eternal life. For God did not send His Son into the world to condemn the world, but to save the world through Him."

Admitted to God, to ourselves and to another human being the exact nature of our wrongs.

5th step in "The Twelve Steps" Program

Great God whose omniscience includes knowing all my thoughts and deeds, I pray for the insight of repenting. Repenting, the act of "turning around," may be the most intelligent, most courageous and most moral act of my life.

When I am pursuing false gods, illusory goals of life, and destructive relationships with other persons, turning in a new direction onto a new road of life is my first and greatest need. This first step cannot be done with my own power. I am powerless until I find power in your loving presence.

In repenting and turning to you, I discover the new day, new birth, new beginning, and new creation. For you "are a merciful God, you will not abandon us, nor forget the covenant with our ancestors."[44]

In the precise moment of sincere repenting, I see the ugly reality of my style of thinking and acting as you see them. This truth is like hard rain in the driving wind of your Spirit.

---

[44] Deuteronomy 4:31

Painfully, it washes me clean. Turning, repenting, invites me to choose "the road less traveled" where new road signs of loyalty, justice, and kindness direct my way. Repenting, I find new companions of the way, including the Master of this journey, Jesus Christ. The reward of faith is new understanding. Once I thought I must understand all things in order to believe. Now, you have shown me that believing precedes seeing, and trusting leads to new understanding. In retrospect, I do have the evidence of what faith hopes for. It is the substance of love, with you, others, and a newly discovered self.

Repenting, turning around, I see the wide horizons of a "new heaven and new earth." The mountains of old nihilism and negativism no longer block my view. I thank you God for the new vision of life. Amen.[45]

---

[45] Acts 3:19-20: "Repent, then, and turn to God, so that your sins may be wiped out, that times of refreshing may come from the Lord, and that He may send the Christ, who has been appointed for you—even Jesus."

SINGING

✤ ✤ ✤ ✤

I wept at the beauty of your hymns and canticles, and was powerfully moved at the sweet sound of your Church singing. These sounds flowed into my ears, and the truth streamed into my heart.

St. Augustine, *Confessions*

Eternal God whose mystery is beyond the reach of all human minds, I thank you for the miracle of revelation. In many ways you unveil yourself to us, especially in the universal expression of music. Music is a tonic for the tender longing in my soul. Music pacifies anxiety. Music lifts up the mind to majestic heights. Your steadfast love and abounding grace create music for our hearts.

When Moses sang and his sister Miriam played the tambourine, they danced to music praising you "the Lord of my strength and my might, the love that leads the people you redeem."[46] Lord, even the story itself imprints a melody of hope in my mind. Deborah sang a song of victory because you guarded her way.

---

[46] Exodus 15:1-20

Mary's soul "magnified" you, the Mighty One, when you chose her to be the vessel of your incarnate joy and love for the world.[47]

When the truth streams into my heart through music that comes from you, I am humbled and filled with praise for the canticles of faith. "In distress I call upon you, and you hear my cry." Heavenly Father, with David I sing: "You are my rock and my fortress. The waves of death may encompass me and the torrents of perdition assail me." You are the redeemer who gives me a song of rejoicing.[48]

Paul sang from his prison cell after a long night of suffering, Jesus sang on his way to Gethsemane and the Golgotha cross because you are the Lord of promise, the God of the history, the Savior of saving love. Help me, though my nights may be filled with fear, or my days bright with temporal success, to hear you in the music that magnifies your beauty. I put my trust in the hymn of your salvation. Without music from you I would be a body without a soul. Praise unto you, my strength and my Redeemer. Amen.[49]

---

[47] Luke 1:46–55

[48] 2 Samuel 22

[49] Colossians 3:16: "Let the word of Christ dwell in you richly as you teach and admonish one another with all wisdom, and as you sing psalms, hymns and spiritual songs with gratitude in your hearts to God.

STANDING

❧ ❧ ❧ ❧

Give me a place to stand and I will move the earth.
                                        Archimedes

As the rain hides the stars,
as the autumn mist hides the hills,
as the clouds veil the blue of the sky,
so the dark happening of my lot
hide the shining of thy face from me.
Yet, if I may hold thy hand in the darkness, it is enough.
Since I know that though I may stumble
in my going, thou dost not fall.
                    Gaelic poem, translated by Alistair McLean,
                                        It Is Enough

Lord of life, the paths of history behind me and the highways to the future before me cannot be compared to the place to stand you have put within me. In the exquisite architecture of the inner mind and soul, I experience the place you live and make me whole.

This day, this place, this *now*, this conscious thought is the fulcrum of faith by which you empower me to leverage the weight of life and move the obstacles to love and serenity.

Today your kingdom comes into my midst. Now, you are meeting me with acceptance, meaning, and friendship. To know you is the cultivation of awe and wonder. My work becomes a calling, my fears are absorbed in love, and my nightmares are turned to dreams.

The mystery of the gift of faith enables me to believe and then to see. Knowledge may tell me I am an infinitesimal blob of protoplasm drifting at random in a finite space of an infinite universe. Small that I am, you call me by name, you give me a reason for the hope that is irrepressible, and you give me a spirit of courage.

You have even caused my questioning spirit to be the point guard of the pattern of discovery. Faith becomes the opposite side of the coin of doubt. Discovery is more joyous than dogma. Your complete love gives us a place to stand where we learn more from our questions than from our incomplete answers. I am standing, standing in awe of you, standing in the marvel of life. Amen.[50]

---

[50] Psalms 119:161 (NRSV): "My heart stands in awe of your words..."

TRUSTING

Nothing that is worth doing can be achieved in our lifetime; therefore we must be saved by hope. Nothing which is true or beautiful or good makes complete sense in any immediate context of history; therefore we must be saved by faith. Nothing we do, however virtuous, can be accomplished alone; therefore we must be saved by love.

Reinhold Niebuhr

The Lord is my strength, my strength and my salvation — in Him I trust, in Him I trust.

Taizé Community Office Book

God, your mercy is from everlasting to everlasting. You are the Eternal One trusting your creation of life, trusting that order shall come from chaos, trusting that redemption shall come from destruction, and trusting that deliverance shall come from captivity.

Thank you for trusting me, trusting that I shall put my trust in you. Fears rise up in my primitive mind. Fears invade from the present world. However, there is a grand boldness in trusting you that overshadows the timidity of fear. It is better, Lord, to be with you in dreaded darkness, than to walk alone in the light.

Day by day I pray that I shall "trust in the Lord with all my might" for you are "the everlasting rock."[51] I have, at times, built habitats of false hopes on the beachfront of shifting sands. The tides of destructive habits, vain human relationships, and the demons of materialism are churned by the perfect storm whose sea swallows my liberty.

"You, Lord, are my strength, my strength and my salvation. In you I trust, in you I trust."[52] God of saving hope, thank you for the chance to change. You have shown humankind that trusting is intrinsic to the power of love. Trusting you, my beloved family and friends; I seize this day with the vigor of youth and the confidence of Jesus who said, "In me you may have peace. In the world you face tribulation. But take courage; I have conquered the world!"[53] Amen.[54]

---

[51] Isaiah 26:3-4
[52] Paraphrase, *Taizé Community Office Book*
[53] John 16:31
[54] Isaiah 26:3-4: "You will keep in perfect peace him whose mind is steadfast, because He trusts in you. Trust in the Lord forever, for the Lord, the Lord, is the Rock eternal."

WAITING

✳ ✳ ✳ ✳

I said to my soul, be still, and wait without hope
For hope would be hope for the wrong thing; wait
without love,
For love would be love of the wrong thing; there is yet
faith
But the faith and the love and the hope are all in the
waiting.

T.S. Eliot

Eternal God, is time an illusion? You have given me a time to love, a time to laugh, a time to die, and you have commanded me to *do* your Word and not merely hear the imperative truths. Strangely, you ask me to *wait*, and to *be still*. This is hard.

Help me to learn the fine art of waiting. I must wait for your will concerning choices that determine meanings and directions in life. I must wait for the comforting presence of the Spirit to overcome the raving thoughts of anguish and despair that assail me night and day when love is lost.

I shall wait for the next step into the unknown tomorrow when all normal routines vanish because of illness. I will wait for your new tomorrows when the present day is covered in the impenetrable darkness of fear. How inscrutable are the ways of human consciousness that entertains thoughts of self-annihilation in preference to wisdom for the soul?

You, Lord, have waited on us, the beings created in likeness of your image. I am a part of the fabric of all humanity. You wait, and we rush away. Thank you for your patience, your mercy that is "from everlasting to everlasting." Take not your Holy Spirit from me. Melt me in the crucible of the crushing experiences of life. Melt me in the fire of pure Spirit that separates the dross of superstition, perversions, and substitutions from the fine gold of love, truth and peace. Mold me in the new image of the new being I see in Christ.

Transformation comes in waiting. You have taught me this: Jesus waited in the desert forty days and forty nights; he waited in the far country away from the crowds, and he waited in prayer in Gethsemane for the final passage and the final victory of life.

Day by day may I wait on you and find

your wisdom before I attempt to take charge of time and history which are in my mind misconceptions. In your mind, Lord, time is a servant of a glorious destiny. Amen.[55]

WALKING

✳ ✳ ✳ ✳

Two roads diverged in a yellow wood,
And sorry I could not travel both
And be one traveler, long I stood
And looked down one as far as I could
To where it bent in the undergrowth;

I shall be telling this with a sigh
Somewhere ages and ages hence:
Two roads diverged in a wood, and I —
I took the one less traveled by,
And that has made all the difference.
Robert Frost, The Road Not Taken

---

[55] Psalms 27:13-14: "I am still confident of this: I will see the goodness of the Lord in the land of the living. Wait for the Lord; be strong and take heart and wait for the Lord."

Then Jesus told them, "You are going to have the light just a little while longer. Walk while you have the light, before darkness overtakes you."

John 12:35

Eternal God, you are timeless, and Lord of time and the pace of life. You are teaching me, year by year, that it is not how much or how long I live, but walking the right road that gives fulfillment to life. "The good die young," but the wisdom and influence of the good person never ends. Thank you for giving our species the art of walking. For some, the physical act of motion is denied. For all persons of faith, "walking with God" gives wings to thought, meditation and prayer.

Abraham and Sarah, and the generations that followed, walked across the chosen landscape to the destiny you called them to fulfill. Lord Christ, you walked through the ancient land with its temple, synagogues and marketplaces speaking and demonstrating the saving truth of life. Walking along the Via Dolorosa, "the way of suffering," to the cross, you began the journey that gives us the road to freedom, if we are willing to walk with you in faith.

Thank you for slowing me down. I was running past life, accelerating to condense time, and speeding to cover more space. Velocity did not lead toward veracity.

Today you were with me in the slower pace of walking, about the same cadence as chanting. I saw a single tiny flower, about an inch taller than the mowed grass. It had been saved by the gardener who carefully mowed around its fragile beauty. It made me grateful for the flower, the gardener, and for you, Lord. You inspire the sense of beauty and value in life. Walking by the grocery store checkout clerk yesterday, I saw the horrible scar on her upper arm, exposed as she placed a bag of groceries in the cart. I had already learned that she was from Rwanda and that her scar was from an unattended wound. What unspeakable violence speaks through the such a scar? Lord, you know her, and I pray that now she feels safe from harm and free in liberty.

Walking and praying help me see more clearly the spiritual steps I may follow if by faith I follow Christ. Amen.[56]

---

[56] John 8:12: "When Jesus spoke again to the people, He said, 'I am the light of the world. Whoever follows me will never walk in darkness, but will have the light of life.'"

EPILOGUE

Prayers have been like mountains marking my journey through the landscapes of life. My mother at the age of eighty-two told me she had dedicated me to God for ministry before I was actually born. She had my two sisters and one or more miscarriages before my birth. The "dedication" was part of her negotiations with God to give her beloved husband a son. I cannot be sure what God's mind was in the matter, but wisely, my mother never told me this story until I had served for decades in the ministry. She understood rebellion from parental dominance.

Prayers were a natural part of my dad's life. He was a superintendent of schools. Without prejudicial assumptions he would pray for the young boys or girls in trouble in the school system as if they were part of the family, and they were. My dad was my friend, so I never had to reject the positive experience of prayer as a form of revolution against the ruling party which is a common part of the transition of growing up.

As a pastor, prayer with people in crises

provided a foundation where someone could stand and face the circumstances that could not be changed, but they could change attitudes about those realities. Prayer is not something a pastor does. It is allowing the communion of the Living Lord to be experienced. Prayer's power is what God does. I saw God change people's lives when they faced death, divorce, depression, disillusionment and defeat.

One of the mountains of prayer along this life journey, and I can still see it in the distance behind me, was related to the "call" to ministry. At a time when athletics were my gods, the extraordinary circumstance of an illness confined me to bed for many weeks of recovery. Before that time, thoughts of a vocation only included sport. Prayer was a part of recovery. Prayer was the primary factor in ultimately following a vocation of ministry in the church of Jesus Christ.

The choice of my beloved partner for life, Joanna, and our family joys, responsibilities, and experiences were all benchmarked with prayer. Seldom did we have wisdom to understand what we must do. Always we trusted that we were never alone.

The most recent mountain of prayer on the panorama was the family experience at Joanna's death; mother of our four daughters, wife of forty-four years. Shock, sorrow, sympathy and love, joy, peace attached themselves to our lives. All of us are grateful for God's mysterious and steadfast presence made real in prayer. The greatest prayer any of us heard was Joanna's, who comforted the hospital chaplain on her last day of life with these words: "Every thing is all right, this (my death) is such a small thing in the greater scheme of God." Even her smile with these words showed us she was in deep conversation with God, the essence of prayer.

The ensuing years have brought new experiences in ministry and a new marriage. My new companion for the journey of life, Laurel, is a witness to the power of prayer.

—Glory be to God—

Personal Prayer Journal

"I will thank [God] for the pleasures
given me through my senses,
for the glory of the thunder, for the mystery of music,
for the singing of birds and the laughter of children...
Truly, O Lord, the earth is full of your riches!"

Edward King

Personal Prayer Journal

_____

_____

_____

_____

_____

_____

_____

_____

_____

_____

_____

_____

_____

_____

_____

_____

_____

_____

Personal Prayer Journal

_____

_____

_____

_____

_____

_____

_____

_____

_____

_____

_____

_____

_____

_____

_____

Personal Prayer Journal

_____

_____

_____

_____

_____

_____

_____

_____

_____

_____

_____

_____

_____

_____

_____

_____

Personal Prayer Journal

_____

_____

_____

_____

_____

_____

_____

_____

_____

_____

_____

_____

_____

_____

_____

_____

Personal Prayer Journal

_____

_____

_____

_____

_____

_____

_____

_____

_____

_____

_____

_____

_____

_____

_____

_____

_____

_____

Personal Prayer Journal

_____

_____

_____

_____

_____

_____

_____

_____

_____

_____

_____

_____

_____

_____

Personal Prayer Journal

_____

_____

_____

_____

_____

_____

_____

_____

_____

_____

_____

_____

_____

_____

_____

_____

Personal Prayer Journal

_____

_____

_____

_____

_____

_____

_____

_____

_____

_____

_____

_____

_____

_____

_____

_____

Personal Prayer Journal

_____

_____

_____

_____

_____

_____

_____

_____

_____

_____

_____

_____

_____

_____

_____

_____

Personal Prayer Journal

_____

_____

_____

_____

_____

_____

_____

_____

_____

_____

_____

_____

_____

_____

_____

Personal Prayer Journal

_____

_____

_____

_____

_____

_____

_____

_____

_____

_____

_____

_____

_____

_____

_____

_____

Personal Prayer Journal

_____

_____

_____

_____

_____

_____

_____

_____

_____

_____

_____

_____

_____

_____

Personal Prayer Journal

_____
_____
_____
_____
_____
_____
_____
_____
_____
_____
_____
_____
_____
_____
_____
_____

Personal Prayer Journal

_____

_____

_____

_____

_____

_____

_____

_____

_____

_____

_____

_____

_____

_____

Personal Prayer Journal

_____

_____

_____

_____

_____

_____

_____

_____

_____

_____

_____

_____

_____

_____

_____

Personal Prayer Journal

_____

_____

_____

_____

_____

_____

_____

_____

_____

_____

_____

_____

_____

_____

_____

Personal Prayer Journal

_____

_____

_____

_____

_____

_____

_____

_____

_____

_____

_____

_____

_____

_____

_____

_____

_____